Dedicated to Hazel, my hero and inspiration.
You are the bravest.

Hazel's Worries

Written by Phillippa Farah
Illustrated by Helen Ayle

First Printing, 2026

Published by Phillippa Farah
www.phillippafarah.au

ISBN 978-1-7635111-0-1 Hazel's Worries Hardcover version
ISBN 978-1-7635111-1-8 Hazel's Worries Paperback version
ISBN 978-1-7635111-2-5 Hazel's Worries Pocket Paperback version

A note to Parents, Carers and Teachers:
This book is just the start of working through a child's anxiety and is not meant to replace the role of trained professionals who can assist with mental illness.
If you or a child need urgent assistance contact:
Lifeline 13 11 14
Kids Helpline 1800 551 800
Beyond Blue 1300 224 636
Headspace 1800 650 890

Hazel's Worries

And how she found
the strength to face them

Written by: Phillippa Farah

Illustrated by: Helen Ayle

Did you know everyone
worries?
It's actually very, **very** normal
to worry sometimes.

Worries can be small and just a bit of a bother or,
they might be a medium sized worry
(which is a little bit more than a small worry),
or some worries can feel **really** big.

Big worries are the kind that are so big they might stop us from doing everyday things and even the things we love.

Do you ever have big worries?

Worries can also be called anxious thoughts......
And anxious thoughts give us feelings in our mind and body called **anxiety.**

Remember, it is normal to worry or feel some anxiety...
Everyone gets it. Even your Mum and Dad.
Even your teachers.

Even your favourite singer or sports player.
and **even** your friends, class mates or team mates.
Everyone experiences anxiety from time to time.

So now that we know worries and anxiety are normal,
what do we do if our worries are **really** big
and bothering us all the time?

HELP!

Meet Hazel.

She is just like most girls.
She loves her family and friends, she goes to school and in the afternoon heads off to swimming or gymnastics.
She loves to spend her spare time making things or reading.

Hazel has normal kid problems.

Like wanting to eat all the cheese in the house (but her mum says she'll get a sore tummy).

Sometimes she has
disagreements
with her sister or friends.

And sometimes she wants to watch TV all day but sadly is not allowed.

Sometimes she wants to stay up until midnight but again, she's not allowed.

And not too long ago
Hazel knew what it was like to be worried and
anxious a **lot.**

Little did she know, her worries
could go from feeling like the size
of the biggest, hugest, scariest
volcano,

to feeling as small
as a teeny tiny ant.

Hazel's worries often became SOOOOO big they would stop her from doing things she loved or really wanted to do.

Her worries tried to stop her:

Going to school
Going new places
Going on excursions
Going to sleep
Going places she loved
and
Trying new things.

Her worries made her feel scared, panicky and sick in the tummy. Sometimes it felt like her legs became stiff or wobbly as jelly. When she was worried she often felt the need to lay down (or the opposite) to **runnnnnnn.**

And her worries made her feel sooooooo worried she would cry.

Her worries always made her think
worrying thoughts about the future........

Do you have worries like Hazel?
You're not alone, worries are normal.

Hazel's worries were really REALLY getting in the way of her enjoying life.

So much time was spent worrying she was missing out on being happy and having fun.

Something had to change.......

So with the help of her family, she went on an adventure to find ways to help those worries not feel so worrying.

And along the way she discovered some tools that **did** help her worries.
Lots of her worries became smaller and some went away completely!

Hazel tried lots of things (you'll never know what helps unless you try some new things).

What helped her worries?

She felt better when she squeezed a fidget. The worries weren't as strong when she squeezed. She nicknamed her fidgets her squeezies and had them in her pocket when she went to school or was out and about.

Hazel also found doing handclaps worked. Either with a friend or by slapping her hands onto her thighs.

Sometimes she booked in Worry Time.

Every time a worry came she would say to her mind,
'Hey it's not time to worry yet. Worry time is at 5pm!'
When 5pm came she could choose to worry but she found her worries had usually all gone by 5pm. (They do tend to go quicker than we realise).

When she was feeling big worry feelings, her mum would remind her they were a wave of energy.

Yep, even worries are a type of energy in our bodies.

But guess what!? Worry energy runs out quickly.

Her mum would have Hazel repeat these words.

'This is anxiety - It is a short burst of energy. These feelings are really NOT nice but they are harmless and they will soon leave.'

A points system helped Hazel face her fears step by step rather than in one big go.

How did it work?

First Hazel chose a bravery award. She wanted a HUGE cuddly toy bunny.

With each little step of facing her fear, Hazel collected points that got her closer to getting that toy bunny.

Mum gave bravery points and Hazel wrote them down on a special piece of paper. She always knew how close she was to getting her bunny .

Collecting points was fun and Hazel earned enough to get her HUGE cuddly toy bunny.

She then starting collecting points for a play date with one of her friends. What would you choose as your bravery award?

BRAVERY AWARD
HAZEL'S POINTS TALLY
DON'T FORGET ALL POINTS GO TOWARDS A NEW BUNNY GRACE
Goal: GET DRESSED 5 POINTS
Points
Score
35
Goal: GET IN CAR 5 POINTS
Points
Score
35
Goal: GET OUT OF CAR 5 POINTS
Points
Score
35
Goal: ENTER ARENA 5 POINTS
Points
Score
35
Goal: SIT WITH SCHOOL ON ARRIVAL 10 POINTS
Points
Score
70
These feelings don't feel nice but they're harmless. They can't hurt me
TOTAL SCOR

Hazel also saw a psychologist - a person who specialises in how our brains think.

They're also really good at helping solve our worries or showing us how to see them in a new way.

Hazel loved her psychology appointments. She talked about her big worries, her week and the worries she'd faced since her last appointment.

Knowing she wasn't alone was so important.

Her family reassured her they were going to help her face her worries.

They encouraged her and made her feel understood. They didn't ignore her worries or tell her to turn them off.

Because with worries sometimes you can't turn them off.

Parents, carers and teachers can help a lot once they know just how big your worries are (sometimes your worries are invisible to others).

But you don't need to hide your worries.

Always speak up about your worries and keep telling a trusted adult until they listen.

You will feel so much better if you share your worries with someone who takes the time to listen and help you.

Bit by bit Hazel faced her worries and lots of uncomfortable feelings. (She found all of the ideas in this book helped).

Most importantly, she found she really did say goodbye to lots of her worries. This doesn't mean she never worries. Remember everyone worries from time to time.

And the good news is, there are lots of things YOU can do to help your mind and body feel better whenever you are feeling really, really worried.

Next time you're worried, think of Hazel and how she faces her worries.

www.ingramcontent.com/pod-product-compliance
Lightning Source LLC
LaVergne TN
LVHW071248210926
848486LV00008B/368
9781763511101